A LIFETIME RELATIONSHIP

LIFE BUILDING TIME IN THE PRESENCE OF GOD

52 WEEK DEVOTIONAL
FOR MEN AND WOMEN.

DR. KELAFO COLLIE, M.D.
SHALLAYWA COLLIE

Copyright ©2020 Dr. Kelafo Z. Collie,
M.D., Shallaywa Collie;

A Lifetime Relationship

Life Building Time in the Presence of God

52 Week Devotional for Men and Women

ISBN 978-1-7355413-2-7

All rights reserved. No part of this book may be reproduced or transmitted in any form or by any means without written permission.

www.shallaywa.com

Published by:

Majestic Priesthood Publication, Freeport, Grand

Bahama, Bahamas.

Email: mpppublications@gmail.com

1-242-727-2137

Printed in the United States of America

CONTENTS

Introduction	9
Week 1 You Have the Strength to Endure.	12
Week 2 Today I am Alive	14
Week 3 The Rock Of My Salvation (Referring to Jesus)	16
Week 4 I Will Stand On My Faith; What Is My Faith?	19
Week 5 Where Does My Faith Come From?	22
Week 6 Why I Should Write My Vision and Make It Plain	24
Week 7 I Am A Son Of God (Referring To Offspring's)	26

Week 8
I Speak Life Over My Life   29

Week 9
I Have The Power To Get Wealth   31

Week 10
Seeking First The Kingdom Of God   34

Week 11
Time In The Presence Of God: Preparation
For A Lifetime Relationship   36

Week 12
Possessing An Honorable Character   39

Week 13
Why The Lord Will Fight For Me   42

Week 14
Remaining Positive During Adversity   45

Week 15
The Power I Have Through
The Blood Of Jesus   47

Week 16
Keep Good Company   49

Week 17
Praying For My Family   51

Week 18
Making The Right Decisions   53

Week 19
Praying The Kingdom 55

Week 20
Demonstrating The Kingdom 57

Week 21
Establishing A Prayer Life 59

Week 22
Worship As A Lifestyle 62

Week 23
Fasting And Giving 64

Week 24
The Power Of Agreement 67

Week 25
Seeking Wise Counsel 69

Day 26
Finding My Role In The Kingdom Of God 71

Week 27
Acknowledging The Holy Spirit In My Life 73

Week 28
Prioritizing: Maintaining Organization 75

Week 29
Respecting Leadership While
Becoming A Leader 78

Week 30
A Practical Proverbs 31 Woman　　　　81

Week 31
God's Grace Is Sufficient　　　　83

Week 32
Effectively Dealing With Setbacks　　　　85

Week 33
How To Deal With Broken Relationships　　　　88

Week 34
Healing After Losing Someone　　　　91

Week 35
Having Gifted Hands　　　　94

Week 36
Preparing For And Maintaining Marriage　　　　97

Week 37
Agape Love- Why Do I Need It　　　　100

Week 38
Maintaining Good Health　　　　103

Week 39
Fellowshipping With Others　　　　106

Week 40
Guidelines To Prevent Deception　　　　108

Week 41
Knowing The Will Of God			110

Week 42
You Are God's Special Child			113

Week 43
How To Handle Criticism			115

Week 44
Living An Acceptable Life Before God		117

Week 45
What About Your Attitude			119

Week 46
By His Stripes			121

Week 47
Obedience Brings Blessings			123

Week 48
Respect: The Way To Win Your Spouse		125

Week 49
Build Up Your Faith			127

Week 50
God Can			129

Week 51
The Believer's Authority			131

Week 52
More Than Conquerors   134

About the book   136
About the Author   137

INTRODUCTION

Develop a daily habit that has the power to transform your life.

Spending a quiet time each day to open up your heart and mind to God will help you start each day with the right mindset, and you'll make better decisions, but above all, it'll heal your heart and will help you develop a healthy re‐lationship with your family and others the way you always wanted. Discover why keeping a devotional is a great idea.

Here's what you will love about this devo‐tional:

* Great 52 Week Devotional.
* It Will Help You Create a Vision Plan for Your Life.
* A Beautiful Journal Design.
* Beginners' Friendly.
* Great Gift for Anyone.

Learn how to overcome an unhappy lifestyle of rush and never-ending stress. Step away from the daily routine. You can find joy and peace, cultivating a spiritual atmosphere to hear God's voice doesn't have to be hard. With the help of this book, you will find new reasons for happiness day after day.

You have made the first step toward a powerful wholesome transformation!

WEEK 1
You Have the Strength to Endure.

Key Verse: "And he said unto me, My grace is sufficient for thee: for my strength is made perfect in weakness..." (2 Corinthians 12:9a KJV)

The world we live in is full of challenges, temptations, and trials. However, the way we respond to these challenges matters a lot. In the midst of all this, what do we do? Should we cry? Give up? Or should we fear?

God has assured us in His Word that His grace is sufficient for us. You have the strength you need in times like this. His Word tells us that "God is Faithful, who will not suffer you to be tempted above that ye are able; but will with the temptation also make a way to escape, that ye may be able to bear it." (1 Corinthians 10:13 KJV)

You may be going through rejection, heart-break, loss of a loved one. It doesn't matter what it is. God has made available to you the strength you need to endure that challenge. "My God can make all grace abound toward you..."

Only make sure your faith is firm on the Rock, be encouraged, don't give up, and don't faint because there is a reward for those who endure to the end.

Prayer: Father, I put my trust in you; give me the strength I need to endure to the end. In Jesus' name, I pray. Amen

WEEK 2
Today I am Alive

Key Verse: "Let everything that breathes sing praises to the Lord! Praise the Lord! (Psalm 150:6 NLT)

Life is a very precious gift. It cannot be bought with all the riches in this world. The reason we must be grateful for it.

There are so many things that could have taken your life. The pains, the challenges, that accident that would have claimed your life, But God has preserved you.

As you woke up this morning, did you acknowledge the Almighty? Did you say "thank you" to Him? Did you praise him with your voice?

The psalmist said, "Come, let us sing to the Lord! Let us shout joyfully to the Rock of our salvation. Let us come to him with thanksgiving. Let us sing psalms of praise to him. For the Lord is a great God, a great King above all gods. Come, let us worship and bow down. Let us kneel before the Lord, our maker, for he is our God. We are the people he watches over, the flock under his care". (Psalm 95:1—5 NLT)

You don't have to complain or question God for the things He hasn't done for you, rather be grateful for the one thing He has given you. He watches over you.

You have every reason to praise God. Come out of that self—pity, don't give in to that sadness, don't worry about what God hasn't done. Appreciate Him for life.

Prayer: Lord, I thank you today for the life you have given me. In Jesus' Name, I pray. Amen

WEEK 3
The Rock Of My Salvation (Referring to Jesus)

Key Verse: "for they drank of that spiritual Rock that followed them, and that Rock was Christ."
(1 Corinthians 10:4 NKJV)

In the Hebrew text, the Rock of my salvation is written as "TsurYeshuati" (Psalm 89:26 NKJV). Tsur is used to describe God as a rock. It speaks of a massive rock that is very safe and impenetrable, Describing God's strength, endurance, immovability, and reliability.

Every building must be placed upon a robust and solid foundation if they are to endure in life. The same is true with our lives; if we are to build an enduring life, we must place it on a sure foundation, Jesus the solid Rock.

In Matthew 7:24-27(NKJV), Jesus gives an illustration of the two builders, the wise and the foolish, who both built houses. One built on the Rock, the other on the sand. Then the storm and flood came, and their works were both tested and tried. The storm and the flood represent the trials of life.

The storm will prove how strong One's foundation is. On our own, we are unstable, shaky, insecure, and can be easily blown away by these challenges. But in Jesus Christ, we are stable, grounded, and saved from being blown away and lost forever.

It is pretty easy to say we are standing firm in our faith when everything is going perfectly well. But the moment we start experiencing rough times, that's when our faith is put to the test, and our response will determine if our faith is indeed grounded on Jesus Christ, the solid Rock.

We can be sustained through life if we daily drink from this Rock, Christ Jesus. This is done by feeding daily in his Word and obeying his command.

Prayer: Lord Jesus, you are my Rock and my salvation. I place my faith in you; help me to drink daily from you. In Jesus' name, I pray. Amen

WEEK 4
I Will Stand On My Faith; What Is My Faith?

Key Verse: "Be self-controlled and alert. Your enemy, the devil, prowls around like a roaring lion looking for someone to devour. Resist him, standing firm in the faith, because you know that your brothers throughout the world are undergoing the same kind of suffering."
(1 Peter 5:8, 9 NIV)

As Christians, we are always challenged in our faith. Sometimes the challenge comes in the form of temptation. The enemy knows exactly when to target us when we're at our weakest, and he knows precisely what tempts us most.

Often, the challenge comes when the world's way is counter-cultural to God's way. We want to be accepted, and it's difficult always to say or do the right things. We are also challenged when we face trials that cut us to the bone grief, loss, sickness, and disappointment can lead us to waiver in our belief. So, when faced with challenges to our faith, God's Word encourages us to stand firm. "So then, brothers, stand firm..." (2 Thessalonians 2:15 NIV).

Our faith is in God and on His Word. "It doesn't matter what happens around us; the Word of God will always remain. "The grass withers and the flowers fall, but the word of our God stands forever." (Isaiah 40:8 NIV). So our faith should not be shaken.

When your faith is challenged, remember that you stand on the Rock of Jesus Christ. His Word is a firm place to stand. He does not change like shifting shadows. He is the same yesterday, today, and forever (Hebrews 13:8 NIV). Dig your heels in and trust the One who is beneath you.

When we are struggling with our faith, Satan will whisper words contrary to God's Word, but we have to choose to cast down those thoughts.

Prayer: Lord, My faith is in you, I will stand firm on my faith whatever comes my way. In Jesus' name, I pray. Amen

WEEK 5
Where Does My Faith Come From?

Key Verse: "So then faith cometh by hearing, and hearing by the word of God" (Romans 10:17 KJV)

When we understand how faith comes, acting on our faith, and receiving from God becomes simple. The Bible made us understand that "without faith, it is impossible to please him: for he that cometh to God must believe that he is and that he is a rewarder of them that diligently seek him" (Hebrews 11:6 KJV). To please God requires our faith in Him; therefore, He had to tell us how to obtain this faith, and how it comes.

"But what saith it? The Word is nigh thee, even in thy mouth, and in thy heart: that is, the Word of faith, which we preach; That if thou shalt confess with thy mouth the Lord Jesus, and shalt believe in thine heart that God hath raised him from the dead, thou shalt be saved. For with the heart, man believeth unto righteousness; and with the mouth, confession is made unto salvation. For whosoever shall call upon the name of the Lord shall be saved. How then shall they call on him in whom they have not believed? And how shall they believe in him of whom they have not heard? And how shall they hear without a preacher? So then faith cometh by hearing and hearing by the Word of God" (Romans 10:8–10, 13–14, 17 KJV).

We see from this text that faith comes by hearing the Word of God. Build up your faith by getting acquainted with the Word of God. Read the Bible daily, claiming the promises of God. Listen to Bible teachings that build-up your faith in God.

Confess the Word of God daily, and let it have a firm grip on you. You will see how much faith you'll have when you consistently feed on God's Word.

Prayer: Lord, help me to build up my faith in you. In Jesus' name, I pray. Amen

# WEEK 6
Why I Should Write My Vision and Make It Plain

Key Verse: "And the Lord answered me and said, Write the vision and engrave it so plainly upon tablets that everyone who passes may [be able to] read [it easily and quickly] as he hastens by."(Habakkuk 2:2 AMP)

Have you ever had a great idea? Have you ever woken up with a great vision or concept, but you couldn't write it down because you were busy. Did you also discover that by the time you tried to write it down later in the day, it seemed that the vision or idea had disappeared? This is because we tend to forget things and an excellent reason to write your vision down.

Thoughts can change things when they are implemented. If it is not written, it does not come to pass. If it is not written down, we can't make blueprints or see what it can become. When we write it down, it becomes a step to achieving that vision.

When you write down your ideas, it makes that idea clearer. The view automatically stores in the brain when written. Also, whenever we write down our thoughts, we begin to see a more straightforward path to achieving it.

Your vision may be a business idea or a strategy to enhance your specialty or an approach to working with others. It could be a potential book or manual or side business for you to create wealth and more jobs. When the vision or thoughts are written down, they begin solidifying.

So, the next time you have a great thought or idea, write it down.

Prayer: As I write my vision down, Lord, help me to run with it and be successful. In Jesus' name, I pray. Amen

WEEK 7
I Am A Son Of God (Referring To Offspring's)

Key Verse: "For those who are led by the Spirit of God are the children of God. The Spirit you received does not make you slaves so that you live in fear again; rather, the Spirit you received brought about your adoption to sonship. And by him, we cry, Father." The Spirit himself testifies with our Spirit that we are God's children. Now if we are children, then we are heirs heirs of God and co—heirs with Christ if indeed we share in his sufferings so that we may also share in his glory." (Romans 8:14—17 NIV)

The Scripture repeatedly reveals that God is a literal Father, and we are His literal children! The word son appears 422 times in the New Testament, at least half the time referring to Jesus Christ. The Word father in the New Testament usually refers to God, the Father. The Bible says God is a Father, and Christ is His Son. So God is a Family!

Just the same way Jesus is a Son of God, we too can become sons of God. Romans 8:14 says if the Spirit of God controls us, we are Sons of God. To be a son, one must first be "born again" (John 3:3 NIV), washed in the Lamb's blood, and be controlled by the Spirit of God. There should be a definite time when you were born into God's family by salvation through Christ.

As sons of God, there are privileges; we become joint—heirs with Christ and partakers of the saints' inheritance in the light. As a son of God, you have power and authority over the devil and his agents. You also have the angels to minister and serve you.

Are you a son of God? Have you been washed in the blood of the Lamb?

Prayer: Father, I know that your Spirit controls me; I declare that "I am a son of God." In Jesus' name, I pray. Amen

WEEK 8
I Speak Life Over My Life

Key Verse: "Death and life are in the power of the tongue, and those who love it will eat its fruit..." (Proverbs 18:2 NKJV)

Your mouth's words are so strong that it can change your life either for good or evil. Our key Verse has said it all. The Bible made no mistake when it said that life and death lie in the power of your tongue. Our tongue is the most powerful part of our body. You speak healing and health to your body with your tongue. You talk to God in prayer with your tongue. You make declarations over your life with your tongue.

In Genesis chapter 1, God created the heaven and the earth through the Word of his mouth. Through the Word of mouth, He brought to being all the firmaments and also made man. In the ministry of Jesus, the Bible said that he spoke to the fig tree, and it dried up, and through the spoken Word, he did many signs and wonders.

Today, Christ has given us the authority to speak life in everything. He said that "we shall have whatsoever we say" I want you to speak life to yourself. Speak life to your problems, your marriage, everything around you, and God will honor it. I know how hard it is to speak life when everything seems upside down, but we need to speak life to turn it around in our favor.

The words you speak will all depend on what's filling your heart. Jesus said, "Out of the abundance of the heart [the] mouth speaks" (Luke 6:45 NKJV). What do you fill your heart with; the promises of God or the problems from the world?

Prayer: O Lord, I speak life into my life today! In Jesus' name, I pray. Amen

WEEK 9
I Have The Power To Get Wealth

Key Verse: "But thou shalt remember the Lord thy God: for it is he that giveth thee power to get wealth, that he may establish his covenant which he swore unto thy fathers, as it is this day." (Deuteronomy 8:18 KJV)

The Bible made it clear here that God has given us everything we need here on earth. This includes wealth, all-round success, etc. Every Christian is automatically entitled to amassing wealth. It is our inheritance in Christ Jesus. (2 Peter 1:3 KJV).2 Corinthians 9:8 NLT says, "And God will generously provide all you need. Then you will always have everything you need and plenty left over to share with others". God is very much interested in our happiness and thus has made plans for it. He wants us to prosper. Jeremiah 29:11 NLT says," For I know the plans I have for you," says the Lord. They are plans for good and not for disaster, to give you a future and a hope."

Why does He want you to be rich! He loves and cares for us. He doesn't want to see any of His children suffer. He has always had our best interest at heart.

However, this entitlement can only be unlocked by us. On our own, we must make every effort. Hard work, diligence, as well as a discipline are significant. We must never be lazy; we must work!

It is His ability working through us, so we hardly have any reason to boast. God has given each of us the power to get wealth. "Now all glory to God, who is able, through his mighty power at work within us, to accomplish infinitely more than we might ask or think." (Ephesians 3:20 NLT)

You've got the power, every ability you need to have, now what are you going to do with it? Do not limit yourself anymore; you have the power to get wealth!

Prayer: Thank you, Father, because you have given me the power to get wealth. In Jesus' name, I pray. Amen

WEEK 10
Seeking First The Kingdom Of God

Key Verse: "But seek ye first the kingdom of God, and his righteousness; and all these things shall be added unto you" (Matthew 6:33 KJV)

The command and promise in our text firmly show how much God loves and cares for our souls. If He didn't care for us or did a little care for us, he wouldn't go on trying to persuade us to seek His Kingdom first. He wants us to take care of our souls; He has promised to take care of our physical wants.

In this text, Jesus demands that everything else is thrown into the background. He wants us to make the salvation of our soul the utmost priority. Jesus knows that we have needs that are to be met. He knows we need food, shelter, clothing, wealth, family, etc. But first of all, He says, seek first the kingdom of God and His righteousness, then every other thing you desire, you shall have"(Paraphrased).

The reason is that there is no amount of earthly treasure or wealth we will acquire that is and can be compared to our soul. Mark 8:36 NKJV says, "For what does it profit a man to gain the whole world, and forfeit his life [in the eternal kingdom of God?".

Hence, there is a judgment for anyone who does neglect to seek after God's righteousness. Such a person will lose everything he has acquired and lose the one thing that he should have sought after, preserving his soul.

Your soul is most valuable; you can't afford to trade it for anything. Seek first the Kingdom of God and his righteousness, and then you can be sure that you will not lack anything good.

Prayer: O Lord, help me to make seeking your Kingdom and righteousness my priority. In Jesus' name, I pray. Amen

WEEK 11
Time In The Presence Of God: Preparation For A Lifetime Relationship

Key Verse: "One thing have I asked of the LORD, that will I seek after: that I may dwell in the house of the LORD all the days of my life, to gaze upon the beauty of the LORD and to inquire in his temple." (Psalm 27:4 NIV)

David said my heart desire is that I'll spend all my days in the house of the Lord because he knew that spending time alone with God will bring a transformation in his life. Time in the presence of God is the best time a believer can have. David knew that spending time in God's presence would build a lifetime relationship with Him. The presence of a strong leader has a powerful effect. How much more significant is the impact of the incredible power of the presence of God.

Your relationship with God is not only established when you go into God's house, but also you can select your relationship with Him when you spend time in his presence under your roof.

Let your prayer time, which includes studying the Bible, be where God meets you, and speaks to you and not only in the church. Let this be the place where you speak back to him. The relationship is in this communion: him to us and us to him.

A relationship with God happens most fundamentally by the Spirit through the Word. Acquaint yourself with the Bible and strengthen your lifetime relationship with Him. Let Him guide you, speak to you, and secure you for eternity. However, do not neglect the assembly of the brethren. (Hebrews 10:25NIV). Always find joy to be in the house of God.

Prayer: Father, help me maintain a lifetime relationship with you by spending time in your presence. In Jesus' name, I pray. Amen

WEEK 12
Possessing An Honorable Character

Key Verses: Philippians 4:8 (NASB), "Finally, brethren, whatever is true, whatever is honorable, whatever is right, whatever is pure, whatever is lovely, whatever is of good repute, if there is any excellence and if anything worthy of praise, dwell on these things.

2 Peter 1:5–7,(NASB), Now for this very reason also, applying all diligence, in your faith supply moral [a]

> excellence, and in your moral excellence, knowledge, 6 and in your knowledge, self-control, and in your self-control, perseverance, and in your perseverance, godliness, 7 and in your godliness, brotherly kindness, and in your brotherly kindness, love.

To be honorable means not disposed to cheat or defraud; not deceptive or fraudulent. It also means bringing or deserving honor. This is the kind of life expected of a Christian.

On the other hand, the character is a spiritual fruit built from our real, godly relationship and commitment to Christ as LORD. Our moral center's fiber stretches throughout our being, embracing and holding together our relationships when sealed as a choice and commitment, not just a feeling or a personality.

Our character should reflect the fruit of the Spirit. The Holy Spirit in a believer makes the believer in having an honorable character that is worth emulating. Luke 6:31 (ESV) said, "And as you wish that others would do to you, do so to them." Jesus Christ teaches us to love others as we love ourselves. This is the true nature of a Christian, as seen in God the Father.

In Proverbs 10:9 (NASB), "Whoever walks in integrity walks securely, but he who makes his ways crooked will be found out." We must develop integrity, where ever we find ourselves. Titus 2:7–8 (ESV) says, "Show yourself in all respects to be a model of good works, and in your teaching show integrity, dignity, and sound speech that cannot be condemned, so that an opponent may be put to shame, having nothing evil to say about us."

Prayer: Help me, Lord, to possess an honorable character that is worthy of emulation. In Jesus' name, I pray. Amen.

WEEK 13
Why The Lord Will Fight For Me

Key Verse: "The Lord will fight for you, and you shall hold your peace and remain at rest" (Exodus 14:14 AMPC)

The Bible declares that the Lord will fight all our battles for us. God has assured us that He will fight for us, and we will hold our peace. When the Lord is fighting our battle, we must learn not to worry but be calm. We must put our trust in Him.

There are reasons why the Lord will fight for his children. This includes the following:

* One: Our relationship with God: "The Lord is with you, while ye be with him; and if ye

seek him, he will be found of you; but if ye forsake him, he will forsake you." (2 Chronicles 15:2b KJV).Therefore for the Lord to fight for you, your relationship with him must be that of a Son/ daughter to a Father. Are you a child of God?

* Two: Our work: (Isaiah 41:21 KJV), The Lord expects you to produce your strong reasons. He expects you to show him your work(s), your projects, etc. Remember Hezekiah in the Bible. The Lord told him that he would die and not live, but he turned his face to the wall, prayed unto the Lord, and presented his cause and strong reasons before the Lord, and therefore the Lord added more years to his life.

* Three: Seeking God with all our heart: Jeremiah 29:13 KJV says, "You will seek me and find me when you seek me with all your heart." God will fight for you when you seek him with your whole heart, and He will defend you from all your enemies as you depend on him.

Prayer: Fight my battles, oh God! In Jesus' name, I pray. Amen.

WEEK 14
Remaining Positive During Adversity

Key Verse: "And Jehovah is a tower for the bruised, A tower for times of adversity." (Psalm 9:9 YLT)

The Bible should serve as a place of encouragement for positivity during adversity. Jesus also encouraged us to run to him for help in times of adversity.

You can only confess positively during adversity if you feed your Spirit with God's Word. 2 Corinthians 4:8–10 "In every way we're troubled, but our troubles don't crush us. We're frus—

trated, but we don't give up. We're persecuted, but we're not abandoned. We're captured, but we're not killed. We always carry around the death of Jesus in our bodies so that the life of Jesus is also shown in our bodies (God's Word Translation)."

To remain positive during adversity, you should be surrounded by believers for comfort and help. Proverbs 17:17 KJV "A friend loveth at all times, and a brother is born for adversity." 1 Thessalonians 5:11 NLT said, "So encourage each other and build each other up, just as you are already doing."

Whatever the problem, have the assurance that God is near to comfort you. He is near to encourage you and help you. In all suffering, ask yourself, "what can I learn from this situation?" Use the situation to get closer to the Lord. Always take solace in God's Word. All the encouragement that you need is right there.

Prayer: Father, strengthen me in the day of adversity and help me to remain positive. In Jesus' name, I pray. Amen

WEEK 15
The Power I Have Through The Blood Of Jesus

Key Verse: "And they overcame him by the blood of the Lamb, and by the word of their testimony, and they loved not their lives unto the death." (Revelation 12:11 KJV)

There is power in the blood of Jesus, which every believer possesses, as we are redeemed through the blood of Jesus (Ephesians 1:7 KJV). The greatest thing the blood of Jesus accomplished for us is that it washed all our sin away, purged us, and made us as white as snow.

From the minute you receive Jesus as Lord of your life, God forgot all the past sins you have ever committed.

We also have authority over the devil through the blood of Jesus: If you know the power and authority you have through the blood of Jesus, I tell you of a truth that you'll not be afraid of anything. The devil knows how strong you are through this blood. Therefore he'll find subtle means to make you feel that you're empty when you are not.

After nine devastating plagues in the Old Testament, Pharaoh still refused to let God's people go. So, God sent a final plague that would smite all the firstborn in the land of Egypt. You'll realize that when the angel of death came that night, it could do nothing to the children of Israel who had painted their door-posts with the Lamb's blood, which symbolized the blood of Jesus Christ. We have protection through the blood of Jesus because "When I see the blood, I will pass over you."(Exodus 12:13 KJV)

The devil cannot hurt you because the blood of Jesus serves as a covering to you and your family. This is the power you have through the blood Jesus.

Prayer: Let the blood of Jesus Christ speak, and be a covering to my family and me, In Jesus' name, I pray. Amen

WEEK 16
Keep Good Company

Key Verse: "Do not be deceived:
"Bad company ruins good morals."
(Corinthians 15:33 ESV)

You can't be friends with the unsaved of this world and remain a Christian. They positively will influence you. We tend to become more like those we hang around. The Scripture says in 2 Corinthians 6:14–15, 17 KJV, "Be ye not unequally yoked together with unbelievers: for what fellowship hath righteousness with unrighteousness? And what communion hath light with darkness? And what concord hath Christ with Belial? Or what part hath he that believeth with an infidel? Wherefore come out from among them, and be ye separate, saith the Lord, and touch not the unclean thing; and I will receive you,"

They can ruin our godly morals and ruin our judgment very quickly, and we can be deceived if we're not careful. It is also much harder to resist the temptation to sin when those around you are already practicing it. "Whoever walks with the wise becomes wise, but the companion of fools will suffer harm." (Proverbs 13:2 ESV).You have been called out of the darkness and into the light, so why would you go back to walking in darkness again? This is precisely what you do when you make sinners your closest allies.

If you want to succeed in any sphere of life, make believers and wise people, your friends. Hang around those who are wise in the hopes of learning from them; to become better than you already are.

Keep company with those who will encourage you to always be at your best. Make friends of intelligent and Godly, so that you'll be both spiritually, academically, and morally uplifted.

Prayer: Help me, Lord, to keep good company always. In Jesus' Name, I pray. Amen

WEEK 17
Praying For My Family

Key Verse: "For this reason, I kneel before the Father, from whom every family in heaven and on earth derives its name."(Ephesians 3:14–15 NIV)

For any Christian family to stand, the husband and wife must always soak the family into God's hands for protection, unity, peace, and godliness. Acts 10:2: "He and all his family were devoted and God-fearing; he gave generously to those who were in need and prayed to God regularly."

The devil will always penetrate any family without spiritual protection. The devil breaks in either through the wife, husband, or children.

At times you see homes that are torn apart, filled with wayward children, irresponsible husbands, and fathers, have setbacks, etc.

Luke 18:1 says, "Now He was telling them a parable to show them that at all times they ought to pray and not to lose heart." Jesus does not want us to give up in prayer, He instructs us to be persistent. Now there is a difference between a persistent prayer and a long prayer. A person who is persistent in prayer does not necessarily have to pray for a long time. Persistence means not giving up.

Prayer is the pipeline of communication between God and His people, between God and those who love Him. A praying family is a powerful family and a terror to the Kingdom of darkness.

Husbands and wives must learn to commit any matter about their partner, which they are not comfortable about, to God in prayer. Instead of quarreling, fighting, or nagging about any issue in your home, take it to the Lord in prayer.

Prayer: Lord, I commit my family into your hands. In Jesus' name, I pray. Amen

WEEK 18
Making The Right Decisions

Key Verse: "Trust in the LORD with all thine heart, and lean not unto thine own understanding. In all your ways acknowledge him, and he shall direct thy paths."(Proverbs 3:5-6 KJV)

Before you do anything or make any decision, always consult God. He'll help you make a good decision. If God is involved in whatever you do, you'll never make mistakes. The Bible says in Psalms 32:8, "I will instruct thee and teach thee in the way which thou shalt go: I will guide thee with mine eye (KJV)."

Every day, make sure your choices honor God. You'll never regret it! We are living in an age where many are consumed with the idea of success & winning. Some will do almost anything to succeed or to win. Ensure that before taking any step, you bring God into the matter.

We must also ensure that we seek godly counsel because "where there is no guidance, the people fall, but in an abundance of counselors, there is safety." (Proverbs 11:14 NASB). Even after careful prayer, diligent searching of Scripture, and rational thoughtfulness, it can be hard to know the right course. So the need to consult someone who has been on the same path you want to go can be vital.

But Jesus is the head of a great Church, and he has put us here to live together. Talk to someone about the decisions or struggles you are facing. It can be a spouse, close friend, mentor, or pastor. You may need to talk to multiple people to be counseled.

An excellent place to start in prayer in making the right decision is to ask, "Does this course of action benefit anyone, besides me?" By so doing, God will guide you in making the right decisions.

Prayer: Father, guide me in making the right decisions. In Jesus' name, I pray Amen.

WEEK 19
Praying The Kingdom

Key Verse: "And He said to them, when you pray, say: Our Father who is in heaven, hallowed be Your name, Your Kingdom come. Your will be done [held holy and revered] on earth as it is in heaven" (Luke 11:2 AMPC)

Prayer is one area in which many of us have misplaced priorities. If we were to consider our prayer lives and what we pray for, most of us would likely find that we pray more for ourselves and our needs than anything else. It is right for us to pray for ourselves and God to give us good gifts, for the Lord's Prayer enjoined us to do so, and it serves as the model for how we are to pray. (Luke 11:3–4 AMPC). But our needs are not the first things to pray for. The coming of God's holy Kingdom should be number one.

The Lord's Prayer indicates that the first thing we should pray for after addressing God as our Father is the hallowing of His name and the coming of His Kingdom (Luke 11:2)

The proper regard for God's holy name is almost absent from the broader culture in our present day. In any kingdom, the subjects must honor the name of their ruler. This also includes the Kingdom of God. That is why; we must come to the Lord with an awareness of who He is and who we are. He is the Sovereign God, and we are His subjects. As such, we must hallow His name.

One way to evaluate whether our prayers are lining up with how God wants us to pray is to consider how often we pray for God's Holiness to be recognized and for His Kingdom to come. If we regularly spend more time praying for our needs than for God's Kingdom's advance, our prayer priorities are off. Let us consider how focused we are on praying for God's Kingdom to come, and let us pray this day for His name to be hallowed.

Prayer: Dear Father, may your name be hallowed today, and may your Kingdom come! In Jesus' name, I pray. Amen.

WEEK 20
Demonstrating The Kingdom

Key Verse: "And He said to them, when you pray, say: Our Father who is in heaven, hallowed be Your name, Your Kingdom come. Your will be done [held holy and revered] on earth as it is in heaven". (Luke 11:2 AMPC)

When Jesus began his public ministry, he did so "in the power of the Spirit, (Luke 4:14 AMPC) and began to proclaim a central message: "the good news of the kingdom of God" (Luke 4:43 AMPC). The Kingdom of God is about salvation, and that salvation spans into every crevice of our universe, ultimately culminating in the New Heavens and the New Earth.

But it started in the lives of the disciples during Jesus' life, and those lives were radically impacted by the power of the Kingdom of God.

It wasn't just "getting saved" in the "raise your hand for fire insurance" type of way. It was radical and transforming. The disciples experienced a "foretaste of glory divine," Storms were calmed, demonic oppression was destroyed, the sick were healed, and the dead were raised. People honestly "tasted the powers of the age to come" when the Kingdom of God broke into this world through the ministry of Jesus.

As Christians, who have obtained salvation through Christ, God has to give us the power to demonstrate His Kingdom here on earth truly. Christ Jesus said, "I tell you the truth, anyone who believes in me will do the same works I have done, and even greater works because I will be with the Father."

Demonstrating the Kingdom of God also includes living righteous and holily, preaching the gospel of Jesus, and living peacefully with our neighbors. We have all it takes to demonstrate God's Kingdom here on earth. If you are not doing so already, ask the Lord to help you to do so, beginning from today.

Prayer: Lord, grant me the grace to demonstrate your Kingdom here on earth. In Jesus' name, I pray. Amen.

WEEK 21
Establishing A Prayer Life

Key Verse: In the morning, a great while before day, he rose and went out to a lonely place, and there he prayed.

Jesus affirmed that we ought always to pray and not to faint. The Bible shows us that Jesus established a prayer life while on earth. Luke 18:1 (ESV), said, "And he told them a parable to the effect that men ought always to pray and not lose heart."

Whenever there is a problem in our lives, or we want to celebrate a big moment, or ease our anxiety, or simply enjoy life, we typically turn to those we love most to share with. But it is even more important to communicate with God, and there's no better way to do so but through prayer. Prayer is simply talking to God. You can talk to God about anything at all! He is our

Father, so we should relate with Him as such. Praying daily allows us to strengthen our relationship with the Lord.

Some reasons why we should pray is One; an established prayer life gives you victory over temptation. Matthew 26:41 said, "Watch and pray that you may not enter into temptation. The Spirit indeed is willing, but the flesh is weak (NKJV)." Also, we have an essential role in determining the measure of blessings we receive from God. When we pray, God answers and opens doors of blessings to us. But we must rise in prayer and partner with Him, or we will not get these blessings.

It is essential to have an action plan for praying. This will help you stay focused and engaged. A prayer action plan will keep your mind from wandering. First, you must realize that you are speaking to a real person who loves you. Be attentive, and focus your mind on the Father who sits on His throne.

Another way we can develop a dynamic prayer life is to have a personal Bible plan. Daily, read several chapters of the Bible. This will keep your mind on the promises of God to you.

Prayer is a Spiritual exercise that puts us in control of our lives. When we pray, we influence a lot of things around us. Even our family, friends and loved ones become positively affected by our prayer.

Prayer: Help me, Father, to establish a dynamic way of talking to you. In Jesus' name, I pray. Amen.

WEEK 22
Worship As A Lifestyle

Key Verse: "I beseech you therefore, brethren, by the mercies of God, that you present your bodies a living sacrifice, holy, acceptable to God, which is your reasonable service. And do not be conformed to this world, but be transformed by the renewing of your mind, that you may prove what that good and acceptable and perfect will of God is."(Romans 12:1−2 KJV)

William Temple, the Archbishop of Canterbury in the 1940s, said, "To worship is to quicken the conscience by the holiness of

God, to feed the mind with the truth of God, to purge the imagination by the beauty of God, to open the heart to the love of God, to devote the will to the purpose of God." Another person, Graham Kendrick, the founder of March For Jesus, also said, "Everybody worships. Whether it is a hero, possessions, success, pleasure, a political cause, a carved idol, or oneself, the way we live and behave makes evident the things we love and give ourselves. It is in our very nature to worship, and that inner drive is God-given; the disaster is that as part of a fallen race, we have replaced the object of our worship. To be converted to faith in Jesus Christ is to return to the worship of the true God, and to dethrone all rivals to His authority. The very heart of worship is the giving, not only of our talents and goods but of our very selves".

These quotes here summarize what it means to worship. Worship is what we are meant for. God has created us to show forth His glory. Our lives, this, must bring Him glory. Worship is not just the singing or praising with the mouth, but with our entire being.

Worship God with everything in you; let your life bring Him glory and praise! Make worship a lifestyle!

Prayer: Let me worship you, oh God, in the beauty of Holiness! In Jesus' name, I pray. Amen

WEEK 23
Fasting And Giving

Key Verses: Esther 4:16 "Go, gather together all the Jews in Susa, and fast for me. Do not eat or drink for three days, night or day. My attendants and I will fast as you do. When this is done, I will go to the king, even though it is against the law. And if I perish, I perish (NIV)."

Isaiah 58:6—11 "Is not this the kind of fasting I have chosen: to lose the chains of injustice and untie the cords of the yoke, to set the oppressed free and break every yoke? Is it not to share your food with the hungry and shelter the poor wanderer—— when you see the naked, clothe him, and not turn away from your flesh and blood? Then your light will break forth like the dawn, and your healing will quickly appear; then your righteousness [1] will go before you, and the glory of the LORD will be your rear guard. Then you will call, and the LORD will answer; you will cry for help, and he will say: Here am I. "If you do away with the yoke of oppression, with the pointing finger and malicious talk, and if you spend yourselves in behalf of the hungry and satisfy the needs of the oppressed, then your light will rise in the darkness, and your night will become like the noonday. The LORD will always guide you; he will satisfy your needs in a sun—scorched land and strengthen your frame. You will be like a well—watered garden, like a spring whose waters never fail. (NIV)

Luke 6:38 "Give, and it will be given to you. A good measure, pressed down, shaken together and running over, will be poured into your lap. For with the measure you use, it will be measured to you (NIV)."

In the New Testament, Jesus told his disciples that some problems would not be solved; some prayers will not be answered except by fasting. Fasting is suffering our flesh to get what we want from God. When you pray, God answers, but you can move God's hand to do mighty things when you fast.

Esther, through fasting, did what has never been done before. She made the king have a sleepless night until her request was granted. This is the power of fasting.

Jesus Christ, on several occasions, encouraged his disciples to fast. He also practiced it before His earthly ministry. Immediately after His beautiful baptism, He fasted forty days in the wilderness.

On the other hand, giving is something that you must—do if you expect your purse to be filled. Giving should be done with a cheerful heart. It must come from the heart and not under compulsion. "Each of you should give what you have decided in your heart to give, not reluctantly or under compulsion, for God loves a cheerful giver." (2 Corinthians 9:7).

After you have fasted and prayed, it is also essential to understand the principle for receiving from God. To receive, you must learn to give.

Prayer: Father, ignite the Spirit of fasting and giving in me. In Jesus' name, I pray. Amen

WEEK 24
The Power Of Agreement

Key Verse: Matthew 18:19–20 (NASB)
"Again, I say to you, if two of you agree on earth about anything they ask, it will be done for them by my Father in heaven. For where two or three are gathered in my name, there am I among them."

From our crucial Verse, we have realized that there has to be an agreement for every organization to move forward. For healing to take place, earth and heaven must agree to the release of power. No agreement means no power is released.

The agreement is vital for anything to materialize. If you desire to heal, you need to agree with God's Word that you are healed. If it is riches, then you need to decide that you are rich. Amos 3:3 (NLT), said, "Can two people walk together without agreeing on the direction?"Lack of agreement can destroy a family or company. You need to solve all issues quickly and move into an agreement. If you are married but not in agreement with your spouse, you will not progress. You should also be in agreement with your children. And vice versa

You might move from one business to another when the problem lies with disagreement. Therefore you must agree. If you want anything you lay your hands on to succeed, you need to ensure there is agreement. When we agree, battles will be won, progress will be made, and lots more.

The Bible has several instances of people who made progress because there was an agreement. The children of Israel crossed Jordan on dry land. They pulled down the walls of Jericho because they agreed. They won several battles because they agreed.

Prayer: Lord, help me to be in agreement with you and with my spouse. In Jesus' name, I pray. Amen

WEEK 25
Seeking Wise Counsel

Key Verse: "Listen to advice and accept discipline, and at the end, you will be counted among the wise..."
(Proverbs 19:20 NLT)

Whenever we talk about seeking wise counsel, we call to mind Rehoboam's story, who heeded to the young men's foolish counsel and lost his Kingdom.

It is always important to seek counsel from our godly elders because they must have faced such situations and circumstances in life and, therefore, would have the right counsel to give the young ones. Rehoboam received counsel from both the older adults and the young men but he heeded to the foolish counsel given to him by the young men.

In proverbs 15:22, the Bible said, "Where counsel (especially from those who know us intimately and understand us personally), is absent, plans are frustrated and break down."

When our perspective is enlarged by input from several caring, experienced, and honest counselors, our plans will be examined and improved until they are established or come to pass. Practically speaking, it is useful to have counselors who know you well, from whom you have few secrets, and have wide-ranging experience in the areas you need help. [Those persons must be of exceptional, uncompromising, Godly character]

Some pastors, elders, and trustees play this role in our lives. Their knowledge of you and their intimacy with the situations you face combine to provide good advice. Foolish are the ministers who do not listen to their wives and assistants. Dangerous are the pastors who do not seek the counsel of their secretaries.

Finally, seek counsel from God. He is the best adviser in the entire universe, and he never makes mistakes. Seek wise counsel today.

Prayer: Father, help me to seek wise counsel. In Jesus' name, I pray. Amen.

DAY 26
Finding My Role In The Kingdom Of God

Key Verse: "And he said to them, "Go into all the world and preach the gospel to the whole creation." (Mark 16:15 NASB)

It is clear from the Scripture that God has a role for us while we are on this earth, awaiting the day when He calls us home to His Kingdom and sets up His Kingdom on earth. While we are on this earth, God tells us that there are several things he wants us to do.

He told the Israelites to do several things (Deuteronomy 10:11−21; Ecclesiastes 12:13). He told them to go and take the land that God had given them. He told them to fear the Lord and walk in His ways. He told them to love Him and serve Him with all their heart and soul. He told them to keep the commandments. And He told them to circumcise their hearts, love their neighbor, serve the Lord, and cleave to Him.

In conclusion, some people say they don't know what God's plan is for their life. However, if we look at the Scripture, we see that while we are living as mortals on this earth, our role in God's Kingdom is to demonstrate our love for Christ by sharing the gospel of salvation to the entire world. We do this by trusting Christ as our Savior and doing everything we can to allow God to change us into the image of His Son (Romans 8:28−31 NASB). By being transformed into His image, we are best prepared to have success in fulfilling our role in His Kingdom.

The great commission has been given to you, and your role is to be a soldier of Christ. Play your part today!

Prayer: Help me, Lord, to successfully carry out my role in your Kingdom; in Jesus' name, I pray. Amen.

WEEK 27
Acknowledging The Holy Spirit In My Life

Key Verse: "For all who are led by God's Spirit are God's children..." (Romans 8:14 NIV)

The Holy Spirit has been given freely to you and me; therefore, you should allow him to navigate you. The Holy Spirit convicts us of sin and keeps us Stainless in Christ. He will work in Christians until death to conform them into the image of Christ. Rely on the Spirit daily. Listen to His convictions, which is usually an uneasy feeling. His leading will keep you from sin and from making bad decisions in life. Allow the Spirit to guide and help your life.

From the Scripture, we learn that the Holy Spirit is God. There is only one God, and He is the third divine person of the Trinity. He grieves, He knows, He is eternal, He encourages, He gives understanding, He gives peace, He comforts, He directs, and He can be prayed to. He is God living inside of those who have accepted Christ as their Savior.

First, we need to recognize that the Holy Spirit is not an impersonal force but a personal being. He isn't an "It" but a "He." By awareness, we recognize the Holy Spirit's presence with us. That could be just a short prayer as we begin any activity throughout the day: "Holy Spirit, I recognize that you are here with me, and I welcome you to be a part of whatever I am about to do." Being aware of the Holy Spirit leads to being attentive towards Him.

Finally, (John 14:26 NIV) So, the Holy Spirit's work within the believer's life is comforting; just the name "Comforter" itself implies one who will be there to plead your case and aid you in any way.

PRAYER: Help Me, oh Lord, to acknowledge the Holy Spirit in my life. In Jesus' name, I pray. Amen.

WEEK 28
Prioritizing: Maintaining Organization

Key Verse: "So, then, be careful how you live. Do not be unwise but wise, making the best use of your time because of evil times. Therefore, do not be foolish, but understand what the Lord's will is."
(Ephesians 5:15–17 NLT)

Priority is all about choosing the essential thing to give us the most benefit and most significant impact. You know what your most important task is, amongst others, carry it out by prioritizing that task. Find your purpose and destiny in the Kingdom of God and walk in it. Ask the Holy Spirit to show it to you and let you along that path.

As Christians, we are not to manage our time the same way the world manages theirs. We must make sure that we seek God in everything that we do. We are to organize our time and plan wisely for the future. There are time management apps that we can download on our phones that we should all take advantage of. If you're old school, a simple notepad or calendar will help. We are to take care of the most important tasks first. We should pray for God to remove procrastination and idleness from our lives. We should seek to do God's will daily. Continually meditate on the Scripture and allow the Lord to direct your life. Everything in this life will burn. Don't put your focus on the world. When you live with an eternal perspective, it will lead to managing your time better and doing God's will.

Always remember that every minute counts. Don't waste time. For you to maintain your organization correctly, you have to prioritize. Among every necessary task, there is always the most important. Below are tips that will help you maintain your organization:—
What does the Bible say? Ephesians 5:15-17.

✸ Seek Wisdom from the Lord.

- Keep in mind that you are never guaranteed tomorrow.
- Don't procrastinate! Make plans for the future.
- Allow the Lord to guide your life through the Holy Spirit.
- Prioritize, organize, and set goals. 7—Reminders. In Ecclesiastes 3:1—2 NLT, There is a season for everything, and a time for every event under heaven: a time to be born, a time to die; a time to plant, and a time to uproot what was planted, etc.

Prayer: Ignite the Spirit of prioritizing in me, oh Lord. In Jesus' name, I pray. Amen.

WEEK 29
Respecting Leadership While Becoming A Leader

Key Verse: "This is a true saying:
If a man desires the office of a bishop,
he desireth a good work."
(1 Timothy 3:1 KJV)

Leadership is the act of influencing/serving others out of Christ's interests in their lives, so they accomplish God's purposes for and through them, God has delegated authority to those chosen as elders or pastors (shepherds) to oversee the church (Acts 20:28 KJV) and serve as our examples (I Peter 5:1–4 KJV). These people do not hold absolute authority but will give God an account for those placed under their care. Therefore, we respect them out of reverence for the source of their authority, which is God himself. This is because if you cause them grief, you cause yourself distress.

Christian leadership is a process of influencing a community to use their God-given gifts toward a goal and purpose as led by the Holy Spirit. While becoming a leader, it is your full responsibility to submit to the authority over you and ensure that your life is in order. A leader is meant to serve not to be served.

Romans 13:1–14 (ESV) Let every person be subject to the governing authorities. For there is no authority except God, and God has instituted those that exist. Therefore whoever resists the authorities resists what God has appointed, and those who resist will incur judgment. For rulers are not a terror to good conduct, but too bad. Would you have no fear of the One who is in authority? Then do what is good, and you will receive his approval, for he is God's servant for your good. But if you do wrong, be afraid, for he does not bear the sword in vain. For he is the servant of God, an avenger who carries out God's wrath on the wrongdoer. Therefore one must be in subjection, not only to avoid God's wrath but also to conscience. ... This should be developed and nurtured at home, then expressed in the community to (Teachers, Principles, colleagues, Bosses [Superiors]) and eventually the entire world, loving and serving others.

To lead others, you must respect your leaders.

Prayer: Father, help me to submit to leadership to lead others. In Jesus' name, I pray. Amen.

WEEK 30
A Practical Proverbs 31 Woman

Key Verse: "Favor is deceitful, and beauty is vain: but a woman that feareth the LORD, she shall be praised." (Proverbs 31: 30 KJV)

The virtuous woman, as described in Proverbs 31, is a woman that knows the Lord experientially. She is born again. These descriptions are products of grace, for no natural woman can possess such qualities without grace.

A practical Proverbs 31 Woman has these qualities:

1. She is Trust—worthy and Dependable, verses 11–12.

2. She is Diligent and Industrious, verse 13–14,16,19

3. She is Caring, Loving, and Exemplary, verse 15

4. She is Strong and Energetic, verse 17.

5. She is Hospitable and Charitable, verse 20.

6. She Rises Early and Cares For Her Household and Servants, verse 21.

7. She is Modestly and Beautifully Dressed Verse 22.

8. She Brings Respect to her husband and Speaks with Wisdom, Verse 26.

9. She is Worthy of her husband's praises, verse 28.

10. She Fears and Reverences God, Verse 30.

Prayer: Lord, I am happy for making me a woman. Help me to be a virtuous woman, amen. Lord, thank you for the women in my life. Help them to be virtuous women. In Jesus' name, I pray. Amen.

WEEK 31
God's Grace Is Sufficient

KEY VERSE: 2 Corinthians 12:9 KJV, "And He said unto me, My grace is sufficient for thee: for my strength is made perfect in weakness. Most gladly, therefore, will I rather glory in my infirmities, that the power of Christ may rest upon me".

Grace is said to be God's Riches at Christ Expense. We are saved by grace and also sustained by grace. There is little or nothing we can do without the grace of God. We were nothing until the grace of God found us. The Scripture said that we were strangers to God, far away from His Kingdom. But "by the grace of God" (as Apostle Paul would say), "I am what I am."

As Christians, we face temptations and trials in the journey of life. However, God has promised us that His grace is sufficiently available. No challenge is more significant than our Jesus; all you need to do is look up to Him.

The grace of God serves as our backbone, strength, and sustainer. We must understand that there is nothing that the grace of God cannot do. We should always pray and ask for more grace. To understand the importance of grace, the Apostle Paul always ended his epistles with a prayer for God's grace upon his readers. That same grace is available today for us, and as we look into Jesus, he will grant us more grace to fulfill his will.

So, no matter the challenge, be it sickness, pain, heartbreak, loss, or persecution, God's grace will see you through. Even if you are weak, Jesus has promised you his strength. Take solace in God's Word at all times.

Prayer: Father, I thank you because your grace is sufficient for me. In Jesus' name, I pray. Amen.

WEEK 32
Effectively Dealing With Setbacks

Key Verse: "Now Naaman, captain of the host of the king of Syria, was a great man with his master, and honorable because by him the LORD had given deliverance unto Syria: he was also a mighty man of valor, but he was a leper."(2 kings 5:1 KJV)

Achieving your goals in life is not always easy. There will be times when you fail. But what will you do when this happens?

Take a look at these scenarios; imagine you graduated from the University with honors. You are intelligent and were soon employed by a big and famous company. You did well and were promoted a few times. Now the CEO of the company and business continues to expand to the regions. You made a name for yourself. You're smart, famous, and rich. But then one day, you felt a pain in your body. It's a terminal illness. You're devastated. All the successes of the past mean nothing to you now. All the fame and riches do not matter. You just wanted to stay alive.

A lot of persons in the Scripture had setbacks. Some allowed the setbacks to eradicate them, but others went on to victory. Job had a serious setback that could have changed everything for him negatively. But he chose to wait on the Lord patiently.

When you experience a setback, know that God is setting you up for a more incredible blessing! The setbacks become setups when you are patient, face trouble with courage, obey God, and stay confident in His call on your life. (James 5:11 KJV)

Isaiah 41:10 (KJV) says, "Fear thou not; for I am with thee: be not dismayed; for I am thy God: I will strengthen thee; yea, I will help thee; yea, I will uphold thee with the right hand of my righteousness." Do not entertain fear, because it has torment, rather, let the joy of the Lord be your strength when going through setbacks.

Prayer: Lord Jesus, give me the grace to handle my setbacks. In Jesus' name, I pray. Amen

WEEK 33
How To Deal With Broken Relationships

Key Verse: "Cast all your anxiety on him because he cares for you."
(1 Peter 5:7 NIV)

The Scripture offers guidance when dealing with the end of a relationship or a broken heart. We can seek counsel and comfort in the Word of God and the love He provides.

Having a broken heart can make you feel alone and as if no one understands what you're going through, but the Bible reminds you that God is always there to see you through no matter how broken you feel. So, if you need a bit of motivation or inspiration to get through your current heartache, take solace in these Bible verses: Jeremiah 29:11, Philippians 4:6-7, Matthew 11:28.

When your relationship is broken, don't bail out on the process, don't take a shortcut, don't get yoked to anything, or put your hope in anything. Circumstances do not have the power to make or break your life. No relationship, no matter how wonderful, has the power to make or break your life. Only God can fulfill your soul's deepest needs, and He does that in the person of Jesus, by the power of the Holy Spirit, in the context of community, rooted in His Word.

There are ways of restoring a broken relationship which includes:

- Talking to God before talking to the person,
- Always take the initiative,
- Sympathize with their feelings.
- Next, you confess your part of the conflict.
- Attack the problem, not the person.
- Cooperate as much as possible.
- Do everything possible on your part to live in peace with everybody. Romans 12:18.
- Finally, Emphasize reconciliation, not resolution.

Biblical solution by Jesus:

(Between Believers)

Matthew 18:15–17 (KJV) Moreover, if thy brother shall trespass against thee, go and tell him his fault between thee and him alone: if he hears thee, thou hast gained thy brother. But if he will not hear thee, then take with thee one or two more, that in the mouth of two or three witnesses, every Word may be established. And if he shall neglect to hear them, tell it unto the church: but if he neglects to hear the church, let him be unto thee as a heathen man and a publican.

(With Others)

Further Reading Matthew 5:20–25

Prayer: Give me the grace —to deal with broken relationships in Jesus name Amen

WEEK 34
Healing After Losing Someone

Key Verse: "So with you: Now is your time of grief, but I will see you again, and you will rejoice, and no one will take away your joy." (John 16:22 NIV)

Grieving the death of a loved one is an individual process. Some caregivers initially feel numb and disoriented, then endure pangs of yearning for the deceased person. Others feel anxious and have trouble sleeping, perhaps dwelling on old arguments or words they wish they had expressed. Sudden outbursts of tears are common in grief, triggered by memories or reminders of the loved One. Even those who are confident that their loved One is with the

Lord struggle with sadness over their loss. Not all people grieve the same way or for the same length of time, but dealing with grief is essential to come to terms with the loss of your Loved One and move on with your life. Healing for all has been made available in the Bible, and therefore those in grief should always remember that Jesus will exchange every pain for rejoicing, and none will take away their joy.

In Revelation 21:4 (NIV), the Bible said, 'He will wipe every tear from their eyes. There will be no more death' or mourning or crying or pain, for the old order of things has passed away. One strong key that can heal those in grief is forgetting the past and remembering them no more. This will drive the pain away quickly.

Also, accepting the loss is the first task. You accept the loss's reality, involves overcoming the natural denial response, and realizing that the person is physically dead. Next, Experience the Pain. In a way, the pain of grief is a gift to us because it is evidence of love. Next is adjusting yourself and moving ahead. The final task is taking the emotional energy you would have spent on the One who died and reinvesting it in another relationship or relationships. Take solace in the Bible and claim your healing.

Prayer: Heal my broken Spirit, dear Lord, and comfort me of my loss. In Jesus' name, I pray. Amen.

WEEK 35
Having Gifted Hands

Key Verse: "Do you see someone skilled in their work? They will serve before kings; they will not serve before officials of low rank." (Proverbs 22:29 NIV)

Whenever you hear about gifted hands, the next picture that comes to your mind is gifted hands by Ben Carson. Ben Carson is a man who found and developed his God-given talent and is known as one of the best Neurosurgeons in the world.

A talent is something that you are instinctually born with that gives you unique skills and abilities. Talent is set apart from knowledge in that it is not a learned behavior, although it can be strengthened and practiced. The Bible tells us that we are all born with distinct talents and gifts that set us apart. When you discover the talents that God has given you and use them to glorify Him, you will experience a full life! Our loving Lord wants us to feel whole and complete, and it is through talents that we can find our unique calling in life.

How Has God Gifted You and What Are You Doing With It? Please think about how God has gifted you and how you are using it to serve the church, serve others, and ultimately bring God glory. If you are not applying your giftedness in these three ways or don't know what your giftedness is, I would love you to seek God's face and begin to apply the gift he has given you. In 1 Peter 4:10-11 (NIV), the Bible says that "Each of you should use whatever gift you have received to serve others, as faithful stewards of God's grace in its various forms. If anyone speaks, they should do so as one who speaks the very words of God. If anyone serves, they should do so with the strength God provides, so that in all things, God may be praised through Jesus Christ. To him be the glory and the power forever and ever. Amen."

The gift God has given you should be used to glorify him alone and not the devil. Are you gifted in singing, drama, writing, etc.? Make sure that God is being glorified in all.

Prayer: May I glorify you, oh Lord, with my talent and let my gift set me before kings. In Jesus' name, I pray. Amen.

WEEK 36
Preparing For And Maintaining Marriage

Key Verse: Genesis 2:24 (ESV), "Therefore, a man shall leave his father and his mother and hold fast to his wife, and they shall become one flesh."

Marriage is a God-ordained institution. It is also the bedrock of life. Marriage is central to God's plan for man. Marriage encircles the spiritual, social, psychological, and physical aspects of human life. It determines whether a person will live happily or not.

Marriage is meant to be enjoyed, as designed by God. For this reason, one needs to adequately prepare himself/herself to get the best of marriage. It is for mature minds and not for children.

Because marriage is God-ordained, it is then essential that you must consult Him for the right partner for your life. This is because, He knows your today, future, temperament, disposition, strength, and weakness.

How do you then maintain a happy home as a married man/woman? Ephesians 4:2-3 (NIV) says, "Be completely humble and gentle; be patient, bearing with one another in love. Make every effort to keep the unity of the Spirit through the bond of peace."As a husband/wife, you have a lot to do to make sure that your marriage is peaceful and joyful. Proverbs 12:4 (NIV) says, "A wife of noble character is her husband's crown, but a disgraceful wife is like decay in his bones." Proverbs 14:1 (NIV), said, "A wise woman builds her home, but a foolish woman tears it down with her own hands." Men are also to love their wives as Christ loves the church. [Point: men need to possess the fruit of love, you need the Holy Spirit to have unconditional love; otherwise you will love for gain or benefit {in a selfish way which will fail}]

The following are some scriptural guidelines for a happy home:

Love— without love, it will be a waste of effort to try to make the marriage work. (1 Corinthians 13:1 NIV).

- Communication— talk, talk, and talk again.
- Submission— 1 Peter 3:1–6 (NIV) speaks more on submission.
- Humility – Ephesians 4:2–3 (NIV)
- Posses the fruits of the Spirit— Galatians 5:22–23
- Pray for and with your spouse. "A family that prays together stays together."
- Forgive— This is very important if you want to enjoy your marriage.

Prayer: Father, help me to get the best from marriage. In Jesus' name, I pray. Amen.

WEEK 37
Agape Love- Why Do I Need It

Key Verse: "Whoever does not love does not know God, because God is love." (1 John 4:8 NIV)

Agape love is the God kind of love. It is based upon a matter of the "will" rather than of "feeling," as demonstrated by our Lord's teaching in Matthew 5:44—48 NIV, where He teaches that we must love even those we dislike and those we dislike we think are unlikeable. Agape love is the fundamental element in being Christ—like (Galatians 2:20 NIV).

There are many examples where agape love was demonstrated in the Bible. Two examples include Joseph's kindness to his brothers (Gen—

esis 50:15–21) even though they sold him into slavery and David's strained relationship with Saul. David had several opportunities for killing Saul but instead showed kindness to him (1 Samuel 24:16–19).

Our Lord and Master Jesus demonstrated true agape love when He willingly died for the unlovable (Romans 5:1–10). As followers of Christ, we are to love the unlovable as well. You are to be like Christ in all situations.

1 Corinthians 13:1–3 (KJV) says, "Though I speak with the tongues of men and angels, and have not to love (Agape), I become as sounding brass or a tinkling cymbal. And though I have the gift of prophecy, and understand all mysteries and all knowledge; and though I have all faith, so that I could remove mountains, and have not to love (Agape), I am nothing. And though I bestow all my goods to feed the poor, and though I give my body to be burned, and have not to love (Agape), it profiteth me nothing."

God says that without His Love, all the intellectual knowledge in the world, all the supernatural understanding in the world, and all the world's faith will profit and benefit us nothing. Without His Love, we will still be empty, lonely, and without meaning or purpose. Love is the reason God created us in the first place. Thus, if we don't learn to love and be loved in God's intentions, we will have wasted our lives. Learn to love.

Prayer: Father, help me to love like Jesus. In Jesus' name, I pray. Amen.

WEEK 38
Maintaining Good Health

Key Verse: 3 John 1:2 KJV Beloved, I wish above all things that thou mayest prosper and be in health, even as thy soul prospereth.

God has promised to give you good health, but you must do everything you need to enjoy health here on earth.

There are Healthy habits we need to keep, which include. Eating Healthy Foods and practicing healthy lifestyles, Daniel 1:15: (NLT) says, "At the end of the ten days, Daniel and his three friends looked healthier and better nourished than the young men who had been eating the food assigned by the king." 1 Corinthians

6:13," you know the old saying, 'First you eat to live, and then you live to eat?' Well, your body is only temporary, but that's no excuse for either stuffing your body with food or indulging it with sexual immorality. Since the Lord honored you with a body, now honor him with your body".

Healthy Thoughts is another: For a person's health to change for the better, it must begin within. It is how a person thinks combined with what he thinks about that produces the condition, and the activity, that we see on the outside. Now let us look at this in a spiritual sense. Mark 7:15 (NKJV) 'There is nothing that enters a man from outside here that can defile him; but the things which come out of him, those are the things that defile a man".

The next habit is to manage your energy. Two things are needed in energy management, Rest and exercise. Psalm 127:2 (TLB). "It is senseless for you to work so hard from early morning until late at night, fearing you will starve to death, for God wants his loved ones to get their proper rest." Exercise well and also rest well.

Finally, brethren, they know their God and claim their promises through prayer will stay healthy. In James 5:14–16 (KJV), the Bible made it clear that if any is sick among you, " let him call for the elders of the church; and let them pray over him, anointing him with oil in the name of the Lord: And the prayer of faith shall save the sick, and the Lord shall raise him; and if he has committed sins, they shall be forgiven him. Confess your faults one to another, and pray one for another, that ye may be healed. The effectual fervent prayer of a righteous man availeth much. When God's children pray, He answers prayer!

Prayer: Help me, Lord, to do everything I need to do to live healthily. In Jesus' name, I pray. Amen.

WEEK 39
Fellowshipping With Others

Key Verse: 1 John 1:3 (AMP) "That which we have seen and heard we also proclaim to you so that you too may have fellowship with us [that you may share in what we have seen and heard], and indeed our fellowship is with the Father and with His Son Jesus Christ."

The fellowship is a mutual bond that Christians have with Christ that puts us in a deep, eternal relationship. When we talk about fellowship, we refer to the relationship we have with other Christians.

The reason we have fellowship with one another is to encourage ourselves. Some people are discouraged because of challenges, are depressed, weak, and are tired of life. They need the strength and encouragement that comes from fellowshipping with other believers to continue. When we fellowship, we also share our earthly gains.

We must come together and share and also feed at our Master's feet. By so doing, we are preparing ourselves for the eternal fellowship we will have with God when we shall sit at the round table. We should endeavor to fellowship with others. There is joy in so doing.

Moreover, the Bible enjoins us not to forsake the gathering of believers, and also goes on to tell us in Psalm 133 that it is in the fellowship of brethren that God sends his blessings. Always fellowship with people of like faith, and God will significantly enrich and grant you his blessings.

Prayer: Thank you, Father, for the gift of sharing with my brethren. In Jesus' name, I pray. Amen.

WEEK 40
Guidelines To Prevent Deception

Key Verse: "Then if anyone says to you, 'Look, here is the Christ!' or 'There!' do not believe it. For false Christ! And false prophets will rise and show great signs and wonders to deceive, if possible, even the elect" (Matthew 24:23–24 ESV)

Paul, the apostle, encouraged Christians while writing to the churches in his epistles, always to search the scriptures to confirm whatever doctrine they have heard and see if they were true. The Bible serves as a guide against deception, which is why daily time in the Word and prayer is essential.

How can we avoid deception when we are not intimately acquainted with the truth? You need to grab your Bible, get on your knees, and ask the Holy Spirit to open your eyes to see the truth of His Word for yourself.

Pray in the Holy Spirit: We need the Holy Spirit, our Comforter, and our Teacher. He empowers us, protects us, and teaches us all things so that when we encounter false teachers, we can immediately discern their Spirit.

Have compassion but with discernment: Some will come into the church, not as sheep, not as lost souls searching for answers, but as wolves, devourers, opportunists seeking to disrupt and infect the church. Perhaps they are not even aware but are being used as a tool of the enemy to hinder the church's practical work to win the lost. This is why the Holy Spirit's true discernment is needed; so we know where to pour our compassion. But in doing so, we must watch over our souls as the Bible said, "Rescue others with fear, pulling them out of the fire." (1 John 5:16).

Prayer: Help me, Lord, to follow these guidelines to prevent deception. In Jesus' name, I pray. Amen.

WEEK 41
Knowing The Will Of God

Key Verse: "Wherefore be ye not unwise, but understanding what the will of the Lord is." (Ephesians 5:17 KJV)

Do you know that not everything we do is God's will? There are some places we must have gone to, businesses that we have done, and others we have taken that were never God's will?

But what is God's will? This was the primary concern of Paul for the Ephesians church. He wanted them to understand God's will for their lives because knowing God's will make things easier and better.

The will of God is found in his Word, the Bible. As we read and study the Bible, we discover what God has for us and wants us to do. People who never study the Word of God can never know or do his will. After we have studied the Word of God, the Holy Spirit comes in to reveal and guide us according to God's will.

Remember that the will of God includes your progress, prosperity, healing, protection, etc., and it covers every area of our lives. Foremost, the will of God is that you have a living relationship with God through Jesus Christ. If you must know and do God's will, you should start by having a relationship with Jesus Christ today.

Prayer: Help me, oh Lord, to always know your will in every area of my life. In Jesus' name, I pray. Amen.

"It takes You being at Liberty to walk in Greatness!

- Shallaywa Collie

WEEK 42
You Are God's Special Child

KEY VERSE: "I will praise thee; for I am fearfully and wonderfully made: marvelous are thy works; and that my soul knoweth right well."
(Psalm 139:14 KJV)

This is the declaration of every saved soul. Every saved soul is God's special child. The Spirit of God affirms this declaration in the heart of the believer. There are times when the prevailing situations bring doubt to whether this is true or not. Even the attitude of some people around you can try to affect the mind about this truth. But you know what, you don't have to live your life by what people say or how they react to you.

The Scripture says in 2 Corinthians 5:7 (NKJV), "For we walk by faith, not by sight," and the just shall live by his faith. You must begin to say what God says about you and feel the way God thinks about you. You are what you declare with your mouth. Proverbs 18:21 puts it this way: "The tongue has the power of life and death." The stakes are high. Either your words can speak life, or your words can speak death.

The Bible says in Isaiah 62:3-5 (KJV), "Thou shalt also be a crown of glory in the hand of the LORD and a royal diadem in the hand of thy God. Thou shalt no more be termed Forsaken; neither shall thy land any more be termed Desolate: but thou shalt be called Hephzibah, and thy land Beulah: for the LORD delighteth in thee, and thy land shall be married". That is what God says about you, and you are who God says you are— God's special child. Believe it! Say it!! That settles it!!!

Further, read 1 Peter 2:9

Prayer: I will praise thee; for I am fearfully and wonderfully made: marvelous are thy works; and that my soul knoweth right well. In Jesus' name, I pray. Amen.

WEEK 43
How To Handle Criticism

Key Verse: "Wherefore, my beloved brethren, let every man be swift to hear, slow to speak, slow to wrath:" (James 1:19 KJV)

Criticism is something that we face every day in different forms. At the workplace, we are bound to face criticism from our superiors, colleagues, or even our subordinates. At home, we might be criticized by our spouses, relatives, or even our children. The same thing can happen in the church, either from members to the leadership or from a member to another. Being something that we cannot run away from, it is, therefore, vital that we understand and know how to manage and react to criticism.

How we react to criticism determines the effect and impact of the criticism upon us. The Apostle James exhorts us today to control how we respond to criticism. When people criticize you, they want you to talk and be defensive, but we should not be like that. Instead, when criticized, we should endeavor to reply with any of these words; "I have heard," "I am sorry," "Thank you," "I now understand." When you reply like this, it makes the critic(s) unable to repeat anything, and it also gives you ample time to think out a better answer or reply to the situation. It also helps put your emotions under control, thereby not saying what might later be disastrous.

Remember that people who keep their tongue under control live a longer and happier life. Manage your critics very well, and they will turn out to become your most excellent advisers.

Prayer: Heavenly Father, I ask for grace and knowledge to know how to handle and react to criticism. In Jesus' name, I pray. Amen.

WEEK 44
Living An Acceptable Life Before God

Key Verse: "For this is good and acceptable in the sight of God our Saviour; Who will have all men to be saved, and to come unto the knowledge of the truth." (1 Timothy 2:3 KJV)

Everyone wants to do something that is acceptable before friends, relatives, co-workers, etc. We all want to live a life that is acceptable before people, but have we thought about living a good life before God?

For our lives to be acceptable before God, there is something that we must do, and it is in receiving salvation through Jesus Christ. A life without redemption is not corrected before God. Therefore, it is vital that we ensure that we are saved from our sins and that our salvation is maintained.

Another thing that makes a life acceptable before God is love. The Bible said in 1 John 4:7 (NIV), "Dear friends, let us love one another, for love comes from God. Everyone who loves has been born of God and knows God." We need to love our friends, neighbors, and even our enemies. A good life is only possible after we have received salvation and the grace to walk in love with others. Is your life acceptable before God?

Learn to know God's will and mind in everything, obey his words, and live in peace and love. These will make your life acceptable before God.

Prayer: Give me grace, dear Lord, to live an acceptable life before you. In Jesus' Name, I pray Amen.

WEEK 45
What About Your Attitude

Key Verse: "Let this mind be in you, which was also in Christ Jesus: Who, being in the form of God, thought it not robbery to be equal with God: But made himself of no reputation, and took upon him the form of a servant, and was made in the likeness of men:" (Philippians 2:5–7 KJV)

There is this saying that our attitude determines everything. Our attitude is our behavior, composition, and how we react to life events. Have you noticed that people with a bad character never go far in life? Do they never reach the zenith of their career or profession? Have you ever considered your attitude?

Jesus Christ lived a life that we all should emulate in every form. His disposition in everything he did was what made him become who he is today. The Bible made us know that he was humble, gentle, kind, obedient, selfless, single—minded, truthful, and righteous [and He is God]. Because of this, the Bible said, "God also hath highly exalted him, and given him a name which is above every name:"

If you ever want to get that promotion at your place work, you will need to work on your character; and if you are looking for lasting peace in your home or marriage, you will also need to work on your character. What about your relationship with people? It will only get better when you work on your character.

Attitude is everything. What you give out is what you receive, and if you have a bad attitude or character, the effect will be negative, and it will significantly hinder your progress in life. Look at the life of Jesus, and dare to be like him.

Prayer: Help me, dear Lord, to work on my attitude in becoming a better person. In Jesus' Name, I pray. Amen.

WEEK 46
By His Stripes

Key Verse: "Who his self bare our sins in His own body on the tree, that we, being dead to sins, should live unto righteousness: by whose stripes ye were healed." (1 Peter 2:24 KJV)

When a fine is paid, the person on whose behalf the fine was paid is free from every consequence they might have faced. Such a person is declared free and pardoned.

Christ's journey to the cross was not just for our salvation from sin, but for the total redemption of man from the curse that came upon man due to the sin of Adam and Eve. One of the curses was the curse of sickness. Before the fall of man, there was nothing like sickness, but God's protection left him, and he became ex—

posed to sickness after his fall. This was why it was necessary for Christ not only to die for our sins but also to die for our sicknesses.

Isaiah earlier prophesied that by his stripes, we would be healed, but after his death and resurrection, that prophecy was fulfilled, and by his stripes, our healing was secured. The Bible said, "By whose stripes ye were healed." You are already healed; all you need now to is believe that it is so due to the stripes that Jesus took for you. He has paid the final price for your healing, and with faith in him, you will experience your healing.

Prayer: I declare over my life that by the stripes of Jesus, I am healed of every sickness today. In Jesus' name, I pray. Amen.

WEEK 47
Obedience Brings Blessings

Key Verse: "If ye be willing and obedient, ye shall eat the good of the land:" (Isaiah 1:19 KJV)

There is always this tendency in a family that the obedient child turns out to become the One with the greatest blessings and inheritance at their parents' demise. Everyone loves an obedient child and can go out of their way to get anything for such a child.

In his dealing with Israel's nation, God had always warned them that if they disobey his commandments, he will turn his back on them, neither will he fulfill the promises he earlier made to them. He made them understand that their blessings were dependent on their obedience to him.

Believers are called and known as obedient children. This means that we are obedient to the words of God and all his commandments. Our obedience, therefore, endeavors us to God and makes us partakers of the heavenly inheritance through Christ. People who are not obedient to the words of God cannot be blessed. Christ said in John 13:17 (RSV), "If you know these things, blessed are you if you do them."

Are you obedient to all the words of God, or do you do some and neglect some? God loves obedient people, and that was why David was exceptional before him because he was to "do all his will." One is you going to be; obedient or disobedient?

Prayer: I decide from today to obey God in every area of my life. In Jesus' name, I pray. Amen.

WEEK 48
Respect: The Way To Win Your Spouse

Key Verse: "Likewise, ye wives, be in sub—jection to your husband's; that, if any obey not the word, they also may without the word be won by the conversation of the wives;" (1 Peter 3:1)

" Husbands, love your wives, even as Christ also loved the church, and gave himself for it; That he might sanctify and cleanse it with the washing of water by the Word, That he might present it to himself a glorious church, not hav—ing spot, or wrinkle, or any such thing; but that it should be holy and without blemish. So ought men to love their wives as their bodies. He that loveth his wife loveth himself. For no man ever yet hated his flesh; but nourisheth and cherisheth it, even as the Lord the church" (Ephesians 5:25—29 KJV)

There is this saying that respect is reciprocal; and that if you want someone to respect you, you will have to first earn it by respecting the person first.

As a wife, your husband might be an unbeliever who doesn't want to do anything with God. You might have been preaching to him, praying for his salvation, and doing everything you think that will bring him to Christ, but have you ever tried to respect and appreciate him in an express manner?

The Apostle Peter wrote to the women in the church at that time who had unbelieving husbands. He pointed out that the best way to win these unbelieving husbands to Christ was submission and respect. Likewise, men should love their wives. This was by the words of Christ that "let your light so shine before men, that they may see your good works, and glorify your Father which is in heaven." Your spouse must see that light manifested in your life, and by your added prayers, you will win him to Christ.

Prayer: Give me the grace, oh Lord, to honor and respect my spouse in a way that will lead him/her to Christ. In Jesus' name, I pray. Amen.

WEEK 49
Build Up Your Faith

Key Verse: "But ye, beloved, building up yourselves on your most holy faith, praying in the Holy Ghost" (Jude 1:20 KJV)

Faith is the strongest factor in life. Without faith, the will power to live will be dead, and we will give in to any challenge. We all need faith in every area of our lives because faith gives us reason to live.

There are times when our faith gets weakened and seems to fail us. In the ministry of Jesus, there was a time that his disciples were very weak; therefore, they had to ask him to increase their faith.

We need to increase daily and build our faith because as a new day comes, new challenges come as well. We need to build our faith by reading and studying God's words, remembering his past dealings, working with us, reminding ourselves of God's great power, and acknowledging our privileges as believers in Christ. We must also back all these up by praying.

The difference between a giant and a dwarf in the spiritual realm is in the amount of faith that they have. Are you strong in faith or weak in faith?

Prayer: Help me, oh Lord, to build up my faith by your grace and power. In Jesus' name, I pray. Amen.

WEEK 50
God Can

Key Verse: "Behold, I am the LORD, the God of all flesh: is there anything too hard for me?" (Jeremiah 32:27 KJV)

There must have been things that we have told ourselves that they cannot just happen. Scientifically, such things can't happen, and at times, we also bring that equation to God. We see some problems as being too difficult or challenging for God to take away or solve.

God was asking Jeremiah if there was anything too hard for him to do. He reminded Jeremiah that he was the One that created all flesh, and because of his position as the Almighty Creator, there is, therefore, nothing impossible for him to do.

Are there things that you have counted as impossible with God? You no longer pray about them; instead, you have turned your attention for help to man; God is telling you today that he can turn things around for you. He can give you the fruit of the womb, open opportunities for you, grant you favor and promotion at your place of work, and prosper your hands' works.

If it took God just a day to create man, how many hours or seconds will it take him to solve your problems? Dearly beloved, God can do, exceeding abundantly, above all you will ever ask or think. Have faith in God today, and he will turn things around for you.

Prayer: Father, I believe in your great power, and that nothing is impossible with you. I pray that you show yourself strong in my life today. In Jesus' name, I pray. Amen.

WEEK 51
The Believer's Authority

Key Verse: "Then he called his twelve disciples together, and gave them power and authority over all devils, and to cure diseases" (Luke 9:1 NKJV)

A uniform or badge of a police officer is his authority. Without that uniform or badge, they will not manifest authority in a way, no matter how bad the case might be.

Before Jesus Christ could send his disciples into the world for his work, he gave them authority because he knew that the devil would demand to see their authority. Without this authority, it will be impossible to heal the sick, cast out devils and demons, and do all miracles.

As a result of this authority, the disciples were able to do mighty signs and wonders.

In the same way, Christ has also given us authority over every situation before us. Believers should not be running away from the problems or challenges that they face. The Bible said that "at the name of Jesus, every knee should bow." We have the authority of the name of Jesus, and when declared with faith, sickness will go, and miracles will take place.

Stop running away from your problems. Use the authority of the name of Jesus and confront those problems, and they will bow.

Prayer: I exercise authority in the name of Jesus over every challenge before me, and I declare them to vanish away in Jesus' name. Amen.

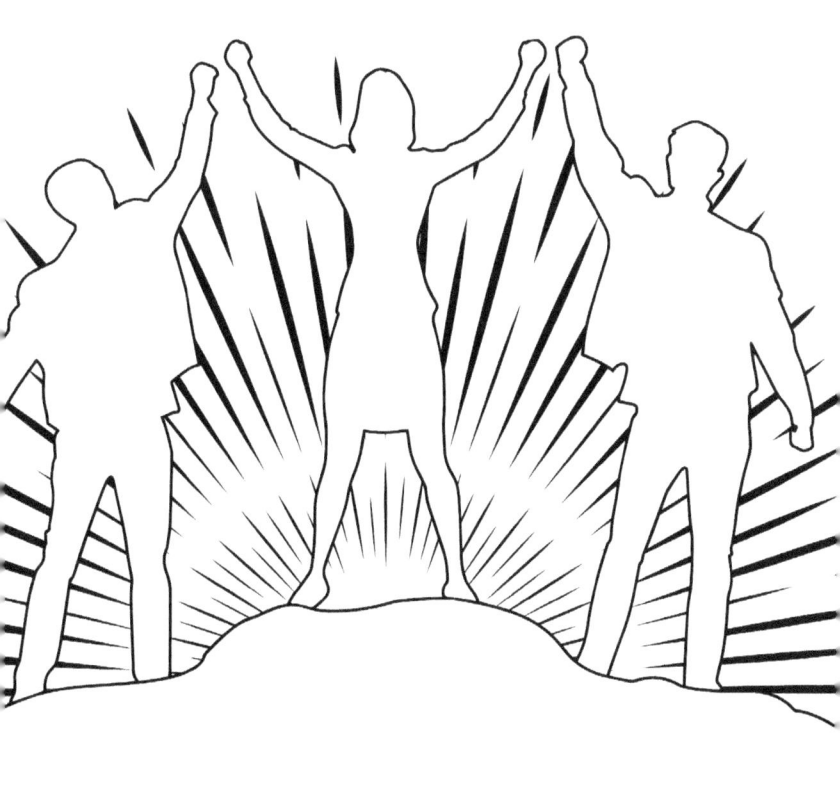

WEEK 52
More Than Conquerors

Key Verse: "Nay, in all these things, we are more than conquerors through him that loved us." (Romans 8:37 KJV)

Life is never a bed of roses. It's full of ups and downs. Some things will always challenge our faith and essence of living, but we must understand that we can overcome and come out stronger despite these challenges.

Jesus Christ knew about the trials and persecutions that believers we're going to face. Because of that, he promised to be with them and grant them deliverance. This made Paul write to the church in Rome that they will surely conquer them despite the challenges before them.

Do you believe that Jesus loves you? If Jesus loves you, will he allow you to be conquered by your challenges and setbacks? Will he turn his face from you? If your answer is no, then you must rejoice because your time for victory is near. Jesus is with you, and he has promised that he will not leave you nor forsake you. He has promised to always be with you in times of trouble and to deliver you, and make you a conqueror.

All you have to do is to have faith in the promises of God. He will make you a conqueror over that sickness, failure, setback, disappointment, depression, and confusion. Daily confess the promises of God and victory over your challenges because you are more than conquerors.

Prayer: I bless you, Lord, for making me a conqueror over every challenge before me. Jesus' name, I pray. Amen.

www.ingramcontent.com/pod-product-compliance
Lightning Source LLC
LaVergne TN
LVHW051559080426
835510LV00020B/3055